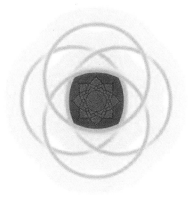

Universal Light Wisdom & Healing Centres

http://universalunity.ca

Ascension Path Work

A Pocket Guide, 3rd Edition

By Joanna Ross

Ascension Path Work: A Pocket Guide, 3rd Edition

by Joanna Ross

Published 2017 by Universal Unity

Calgary, Alberta

Universal Light Wisdom & Healing Centres   http://universalunity.ca

Copyright © Joanna Ross

Cover artwork and design © 2017 by Cameron Gray

Discovering the Cosmic Consciousness

http://parablevisions.com

Facebook - CameronGrayTheArtist
Instagram - @ParableVisions
Twitter - @Parabola

Layout and editing by Linda Bolton-Holder

Printed in the United States

First Universal Unity edition: 2015

ISBN-13: 978-1546498599

ISBN-10: 1546498591

Endorsements

I AM so grateful to Joanna for showing up in my life when I needed to connect the dots and I was missing one. She enabled me to see the dot I was missing and it was a big one. It was reconciling my Love for my Light Bodies, my Christed Consciousness, my energetic self, with my Love for my physical self, which I was in lack of. That was the piece of Self-Love, of loving myself, that was missing.

In this challenge — which in counting numbers, has a couple more days — I have discovered that deeper Love which has led to such a profound awareness and understanding that just as I AM One with Source, I AM One with my physical body, with every cell. As I strengthen that bond every day, I awaken to the miracle of knowing I can truly affect change within the physical as I can affect change in my consciousness.

It is all possible with LOVE ~ unconditional Love of Self. This is my story and it will continue long after this writing is complete this day.

Thank you, Joanna! I Love you as I Love myself!

We are all Profound Source! And So It Is!"

So much Love, Keenara

I would say that the last four weeks have been magical! You came into my life at the moment when I needed so many answers and I received from you such validation. Such enlightened guidance, just what my Soul needed to hear!

The practice of the Path of Enlightenment work. The daily path that we need to do. Going within and tuning into that part of me that is that Inner Light, that Inner Sound, giving me once again the hope and the feeling that I do belong and that I am a wonderful Soul in search of my own identity so I may reunite with Source. As I practice my daily meditation without expectations and with a heart full of love and gratitude to all that is around me, loving vibrations and magical moments start to happen. My inner eye starts to open and I am able to enjoy the beauty of Heaven right here on Earth.

Unless you become as a Child you cannot enter the Kingdom of Heaven.

I have felt that and heard that from within me. Everything is clicking, this makes sense. Purity of heart and purity of Soul is what will allow for this level of consciousness to allow me to see that I am in Heaven. So there is plenty of work to do. Finding me has been my Life Path! Once again I am heading HOME!!"

Love and Light,

Elena Starbuck

Dedication

This book is dedicated to Gaia and Humanity. May we remember the delicate dance that we are entangled within, and may we light the way for greater brilliance and awareness as One.

Preface

Awareness is consciousness, and consciousness is awareness.

In overwhelming response to all the incredible new awakenings upon Gaia, including yours, dear lighted ones, a surge in electromagnetic energy is spurring an even greater potential for others to seek their own light and join in the awakening. This planetary awakening and ascension is a pure example of the *snowball effect*; however, this time we will call this the *illuminated galactic human effect*. Humanity has had so much hidden from us, since the beginning of life upon Earth, but now we are ready to step up into our *new truth*. There is no force that can hold us back, hold us down, and keep our human illumination from moving and expanding.

The ways in which humanity can tap into the unlimited and infinite potential of our cosmic consciousness is not as complex and intimidating as one might think. Daily practice and devotion to being your truest, lightest, most authentic self is possible with every breath you take. Now is the time to allow the magic to unfold, the miracles to flow forth, and your most profound aspect to surface in these truly magnificent times. From our most ancient of wisdom tablets, the masters have taught us about the profundity of seeking within. The self-knowing process is infinite, enlightening, awakening, and even unbelievable at times. It is a lifelong path that allows us to experience and emulate what most believed only to be possible in dreams or fairy tales. This euphoric state of being, this state of aliveness is truly possible for us all, but to live every day as illuminated galactic humans requires that we alter, refine, expand, and explore all that we are. Ascension path work is a daily, hourly, moment-for-moment process.

This quick and simple *Ascension Path Work Pocket Guide* is to help you in your journey of exploration. In these pages, we will review the importance of grounding in these tremendously accelerating times. We will offer our own personal *White Light Prayer & Invocation* that you can freely use and even adapt to your own specific path work and healing needs. We will explain why these simple, sacred tasks of self-love can enhance and assist you in your ascension and expansion journey, as you explore the spirit within. Remember, we are here to experience the process of moving beyond limitation and rise into our unlimited human potential.

There is new life, new potential, and new light within every breath. All that will unfold will create profound new truths that will inspire, empower, and ignite the infinite Source glow within each of us. For it is your birthright!

Contents

Introduction 1
  Benefits of Daily Ascension Path Work 1

Evolutionary Lessons 5
  Self-Love and Self-Honour 5
  Our Physical Incarnation 7
  Healing Ourselves 7
  Healing Gaia 9
  Cosmic Unification 10

Introduction to Path Work 13
  Awakening 13
  Know Thyself 14
  Grace 15
  Connecting and Community 16
  My Introduction to Path Work 19

Preparation for Path Work 21
  Sacred Space 21
  Sacred Time 22
  Unconditional Love 22
  Grounding 23
  Connecting the Sacred and the Mundane 24

Ascension Path Work 25
  Intention Setting 26
  Breathing and Grounding 27
  Prayer and Invocation 29
  Desires 30
  Interacting with Multidimensional Beings 30
  Lessons in Every Experience 31
  Time for Reflection 32
  Uncomfortable Lessons 33
  Shadow Experiences 33

Prayers and Invocations 35
  White Light Prayer 35
  Invocation to Ask for Healing 36
  Invocation to Claim Your Birthright 37
  Invocation of Surrender 38
  Sacred Temple Teachings 39
  Creating Your Own Invocations 40

Our Divine Destiny 43

Trust in the All..43
The River of Life 44
Divine Loving Flow 45
A New State of Illumination...46

A New World 49
Honour Your Inner Temple 49
Find Your Authentic Voice 49
Tuning into Your Unique Vibration...50
Revealing Your Sacred Gifts..52
A New Way of Living...52
Be Inspired to Play 53
Be Your Authentic Self..54

About the Author...56

Universal Unity 59
Higher Vibrational Learning and Ascension Offerings 59
Private Intuitive Sessions..59
Universal Unity Radio..60
Children of Light 60
Private & Group Events..61
First Conscious Contact 61

Other Books by Joanna Ross..65

Introduction

Benefits of Daily Ascension Path Work

The benefits and blessings that daily inner path work offers are much more than one simple pocket guide can explore. We will, however, outline in general what many have experienced as they commit to altering their state of knowing by devoting time and honour, in every day, to a greater awareness and self-knowing. These Ascension path work guidelines can be used at any time throughout one's day and they offer more benefits than what appears on the surface.

As we explore our grander multidimensional potential, we will begin to sense that we are much more than we ever thought and more than we were ever taught. We are infinite beings of Divine light and Divine expansiveness, and in this, the path to knowing *thyself* is infinite. Regardless of what level, stage, or awareness phase you feel you resonate in, there is always more inner work to be done. For in every moment, our earthly canvas is being altered, shifted, and aligned so the evolving human can step into the unimaginable. In every new moment, we experience a new earthly realm and become a new ascending and expanding earthly human. Never before have we known these frequencies while in a physical state of being human. We are literally the students and teachers for all of Creation to see how a 3rd dimensional planetary ascension can be accomplished. These are truly uncharted territories, and, therefore, it is important to go within and seek the infinite wisdom, intelligence, and love that exists in all that we are and in all that we exist within.

As you commit and devote sacred time and sacred space for your path work, you will set the stage with intent and beauty for this grand scheme of inner knowing exploration. Intention is the vibration you set as you move into every day to facilitate trust, wisdom, and allowance to create and manifest all that you desire and value. This process is a delicate balance of quantum energy that requires devotion to regular practice with Spirit, your teams, your Higher Self, and your spirit guides.

Remember, dear lighted ones, all you experience in your outside reality is really a reflection of what is moving within you at a vibrational state of existence. Your reality experience will shift in communion and in symbiotic resonance with the inner work you commit to. We are entangled and enmeshed at a quantum level and the *All* is affected by every small and seemingly minor change. Just as your external reality will shift and alter, so too will your physical vessel, and so too shall our planetary vessel. There is nothing that we are not entangled with. Every change, every modification, will reverberate to Creation and create an equal shift.

As within, so without.

(Hermes Trismegistus)

Daily Inner Path Work will benefit you in so many ways with:

☼ A greater understanding for self by imbuing ourselves with self-love and self-honour through a process of self-exploration.

☼ A greater and expanded self-awareness.

☼ A greater confidence through knowing thyself.

☼ A greater alignment to your soul blueprint and your spiritual, creative offerings that you planned for yourself, Creation, and the All That Is.

☼ The development of a practiced intent to be still, silent, and present with God, thus recognizing, nurturing, and honouring a partnership and loving relationship with God.

☼ Improved health and fitness as all aspects of your inner and outer realities come into balance.

☼ Reduced stress levels, balance, wellness, and harmony.

☼ A greater understanding about Creation, Universal balance, existence, and our role within it all.

☼ Expanded thought as your inner path work facilitates an enhanced connection with the Higher Self — the gate-keeper to all Universal wisdom that is held within.

☼ Heightened creativity when the work promotes a greater flow with Spirit, which is the essence of all creative work.

☼ A greater alignment with those in your soul family as aligned vibrations allow for synchronistic and symbiotic pairing and communion.

☼ A greater alignment with those with whom you desire a soulful loving relationship with such as your soul mates and other Divine compliments.

☼ Alignment with your true gifts and skills for career, joy, success, and abundance.

☼ The release of all fear-based beliefs and limitations.

☼ A healthy and sustainable planet as we all gain a greater alignment, respect, and love for all life in Wholeness, Unity, Oneness.

☼ A diminished reliance on sleep as we integrate a greater light and refinement to allow for a greater capacity for knowledge, wisdom, health, and movement as we ascend into a more refined crystalline human form.

☼ An integration of ancient skills and wisdom through Akash Activations that will ultimately modify our DNA and our physical forms.

☼ An enhanced capacity for communication, love, and communion with celestial and star families, Higher Self, and spirit guides.

There are more attributes and benefits that will unfold as each of us commits to a regular practice of grounding, celebration, and communion with Spirit. The symptoms and experiences will vary for each person, but what is the same for all of us is that our paths are forever moving and shifting. Remember to be patient and loving in your path work and let go of all expectations. Spirit is a free-flow of the infinite loving rapture of Source and there are no boundaries or rules that can contain or control it despite what the ego-mind would have you think. The path to profound inner knowing, self-love, and aspects of the highest and most Divine, are within each of us. It is a delicate and elegant dance with Source, Creation, and all that we are. Listen, tune in, trust, allow, and surrender into your innate brilliance and expansiveness.

Enjoy dear lighted ones, for there is a lesson and a Divine offering within each moment. Your existence is not a coincidence. You are purposeful, you are needed, and your path is just beginning. Welcome to the 5th dimension. It's time to dance!

Joanna Ross

I

Evolutionary Lessons

So many of us have a profound sense that our reality is shifting and moving to something that is much greater than we have ever experienced before. There are moments of great fluidity and elasticity revealing to us that our world is not what we thought it was and that everything we have been taught about reality is false. There are many among us who can feel these subtleties although there are just as many who are completely unaware of these changes. Either way, just know that as we move into the final phases of this planetary ascension, it will become more evident that everything is evolving to align to an increasingly expansive, collective consciousness. As we gain a greater understanding for all that we are, as unique human-spiritual beings, we will be able to better embrace an understanding of our grander entanglement and all that we exist within.

Many souls have been on this path of awakening for some time, and now that so many more are awakening, we have been able to identify and label the variety of phases and shifts associated with planetary ascension. There are two important evolutionary lessons for humanity that are guiding this process. First, we must understand and incorporate active states of self-love and self-knowing (of our multidimensional humanness). Secondly, we must seek a greater knowledge about our inherent cosmic place within the *All That Is* by coming to understand how our planetary collective (both human and other life forms), our planetary spirit (Gaia) and her needs and offerings, and our Universal existence in which we all belong are connected and entangled.

Humanity's Evolutionary Lessons begin with Self-Love, Self-Knowing, and acknowledging our Cosmic Placement.

Self-Love and Self-Honour

When we allow ourselves to create a deeper sense of self-honour and self-love about our humanness in this physical manifestation, what we experience will become more fluid as well as purely magical and exquisitely enchanting.

Never before has humanity seen the level of consciousness awareness that is being activated on Earth, due to Gaia's planetary ascension. Human history has seen pockets of ascended shamans, groups of cultures, and tribes, and even during segments of thousands of years with advanced cultures, but she has never cradled the awakenings at such a profound mass level as is occurring right now. We are seeing these mass awakenings due to the planetary ascension agenda for Gaia and the accelerated final phases that we are stepping into. Our planet, our Gaia, and the collective of all of humanity are sewn within the agenda for a grander Universal evolution. Even if you do not know, at this point, how you and your soul blueprint will contribute to this grand plan, know that you are intimately sewn within Gaia's ascension into 5th dimensional webbing.

Remembering the importance of self-love is the catalyst to our reconnection with our cosmic family, galactic Oneness, and Universal Unity. This reconnection means we will, once again, glow with profound illumination of grace, self-honour, and a deeper sense of love for our physical being-ness as we move through these accelerated awakening times. We cannot express honour, love, and respect for other planetary life forms if we are asleep and disconnected to all that we exist within here upon Gaia. It is an integral aspect of our ascension to move into a state of love with all that we are, with all that we exist within, and with all that our planet is and offers us before we can begin to explore and expand into the neighbouring cosmos.

Thankfully, the human collective is changing with every breath and there are millions of humans eager for this change as they are aching for greater fulfilment, greater intimacy, and greater freedom for everyone. So many want to be free to live and to create a unique life expression that mirrors exhilaration and freedom of spirit. Take the time and go deep within yourself and seek the answers and energetic wisdom about what is unfolding. Learn to *know thyself* and you will unveil the light of Source within you that desires entanglement and re-engagement with all that we exist within. It is our natural drive, our natural force to be One, to be united with All That Is.

We are Divine sovereign beings of light, wisdom, intelligence, and unique creative expressions. This moment of now is the one that holds all of our potential and, in this, there is nothing that we are not capable of experiencing and creating. Allow your inner light, your inner brilliance, and your creative expression to come forth with unconditional love so your lighted path and unique expression can unfold as it should.

Surrender into your multidimensional brilliance, fall in love with your physical vessel and all that it gifts to you. This connection between our expansive spirit, the heightened human vessel, and that of all that we exist within is begging to be acknowledged. All aspects of all that we are, not only carry us through every Earthly moment, but each aspect provides us with opportunities to refine our frequencies to an ever-evolving energetic environment and our cosmic heritage. These are all truths to our 5th dimensional reality unfolding before our eyes and within our hearts.

Our Physical Incarnation

The physical aspect of our reality is the very attribute that intrigued many of us to incarnate in these profound times of change and this attribute is an important part of the Divine plan. Creating a moment-for-moment presence within our bodies — bodies that are evidently working very hard to keep up with a dramatically changing environment — is a blessing and gift in and of itself. We will see how important it will be to engage, value, and appreciate our physical vessels as we learn how to attune our bodies to the ever-changing energy streams and learn to value all that we are. These lessons will allow us to reach greater depth and allowance to the magical aspects offered to us, from the Divine. We will be re-learning and remembering how to truly enjoy the Divine gifts of magic that are offered in our moment-for-moment life experience as vessels of ascending humans. You will discover that it is increasingly important to create an innate awareness of all the moments that we truly enjoy in our physical aspect of our earthly reality experience.

Our physical bodies are unique as they allow us to be grounded in experiences and increase our awareness of the interconnectedness of absolutely everything. Every human moment is truly special and each moment and experience will serve to remind us how utterly magical our uniqueness is as we contribute to create a whole new level of reality experience for ourselves, for everyone else, and for Gaia.

Healing Ourselves

Illness and disease will eventually subside as we go within and heal ourselves with loving care and respect for ourselves, each other, and our planet. We are linked, we are connected, and we are One. As we heal within, we simultaneously heal our earthly experience and world canvas. Every moment and breath that you imbue with the essence of new life, with the vigour and fervour of what Source essence offers, opens, expands, heals, and also creates opportunities for others to be activated by the quantum light so that they too can be part of the healing experience. The self-love that we seek and the self-knowing that awakening requires is our Universal Unity calling for us to reengage before it is too late.

We are awakening to the intricate balance and elegance that we hold within all that we are, with our planet, with all of Gaia's offerings, and with each other and All That Is. Balance and harmony is sweeping across our planet on a cosmic wind, inspiring humanity to reengage in order to assure there will be future generations of our species.

Remember what it feels like to be in love? Remember the sense of excitement you felt when you became entangled with that one person or passion that ignited the depths of your soul in ways that left you completely breathless? *Fall back in love* with all that *you* are, dear lighted ones, for this is the key to a healthy and lasting life. Reconnect in loving and respectful ways with your vessel, talk to your cells, align every morning with the light essence of all that you are and emit loving direction for your cells to move into health, youthfulness, and vivacity. Own all aspects of your reality, for you are a master within it all.

Own what you experience with your body, with your planet, with your environment, and even with your career. Seek the wisdom that exists within and *be* your finest whole self. We must align with all that we are and we must understand what we are based on sacred self-reflection, not on messages bombarding us through the media. We must acknowledge and own all that we have created and manifested so that we can hone our energy to a more enlightened effect and reality experience.

We are expansive, Divine, and profound light beings who are here for a limited time in order to experience the blessings of cosmic and Source benevolence. These blessings are gifts to help us discover our place within an expansive family; a family who has long cradled us in hope and knowingness that this awakening would help bring humanity to an unprecedented level of awareness.

Healing Gaia

We are connected to everything in the cosmos and everything in the cosmos is connected to us. We are all one. Our existence with Gaia, with Earth, with the cosmos, and with Source is a symbiotic relationship and it has always been so. The misinformed belief that we are separate from All and that our planet is here to serve us has created drastically limiting conditions. Furthermore, our collective ignorance of our connection to Gaia has resulted in devastating toxicity and degradation on our Earth that requires immediate attention as our future on the planet is in jeopardy. It is time to wake up and pay attention. Gaia is suffering and it is our fault.

The refined ascension streams that are returning to us as a result of our awakening are inspiring so many — even those who are not yet fully aware that they are experiencing triggers to awaken — to do what is necessary to correct, heal, and work to address the global lack of regard that has led to this dreadful state of devastation.

For our Gaia, our planet, our water, our air, our soil, and our trees are all aspects of all that we are and we must now pay attention to how enmeshed we truly are with everything about us. Our planet is a direct reflection of who we are as a collective. It reflects to us what we know about ourselves and what we feel about ourselves. Gaia is an evolving body that is currently struggling to survive as the vast majority of people living here have little understanding of the greater consequences related to our abuse of this planet and its resources.

To have a better understanding of how we impact All within Creation, we must go within. As we do, our teams will show us how all that we do affects everything else. Once we know this, we will no longer be able to pretend that how we behave toward others and Gaia does not affect the whole. Ascension allows us to seek inner wisdom, intelligence, cosmic belonging, and our deepest Source heritage to inspire us by igniting self-love and a greater awareness that we are One with the All. In this process of self-awareness and expansion, we can begin to heal the great injustices done to all life upon Earth.

Acknowledgement is key and awakening is the first step in better understanding all that we exist within. Walking with a lighter step is a good start. Every thought, every word, every action, and every deed has an impact upon the whole. Never underestimate your presence and what you put out to the Universe.

We are awakening to a greater quantum discernment and acknowledgement so we can create a loving intent to be effective stewards of our planet once again. As we seek within and explore the infinite aspects of all that we are, we gain greater compassion, love, and respect. This, in turn, ignites us as a collective to move away from existing as a self-serving humanity, to one that inspires honour for serving the greater good of all.

We begin with self-healing and as we heal from within we will also heal our outside reality. This healing process moves us into the awareness of great joy, bliss, and an appreciation that serves our evolving spiritual aspects and the environment in which we exist.

The evolving human lives within a multidimensional reality, but the planet we live on is in need of profound care and attention if we are to continue to persist here. As we remember how to reconnect and engage with our multidimensional aspects we will learn how to develop a new way of living on and with this wonderful planet. Awakening sparks our potential to love all the sacred vessels that support us, our bodies and our precious Gaia.

Cosmic Unification

Our individual and collective desire for greater unification and soulful engagement with the cosmos is a quantum reaction catalyst that will move out to the All. Once there, our desires will link to other like vibrations and create entangled experiences that will return to us. The essence of the All is one that craves growth, expansion, evolution, unification, and Oneness and right now we are all awakening to this grand and elegant scheme.

Awaken, dear lighted ones, for it will dazzle and delight you in every way. We are ascending humans as we seek the intricacies and wisdom within ourselves, then work to unify these concepts with balance and grace. Moving through the process of ascension with daily path work is of no use if we do not make all that we are expanding into part of our daily experience and ground new heightened ways of living into our ever-changing reality. The illuminated galactic human is one that not only innately craves cosmic unification, but also intimately understands the entanglement of our physical reality in which we exist right now.

Love your whole self, love our planet and all that She offers, love thy brother, thy sister, and love all that exists. Love thy stars, love thy heart that beats to the unconditional loving rhythm of Gaia's desire for peace, respect, and harmony. We are all united in a merging of spirit dedicated to healing the many soul fragments that are bruised and broken because of fearful beliefs and disturbing lifetime experiences.

We are finally remembering to love our bodies in such a way that we honour *thyself* and ascend to a heightened level of being. We are waking the seed of Adam to ignite our memories of entanglement with the All, our planet, and our cosmic family. There are so many attributes finally coming together so that we may know for the first time in eons how it truly feels to be whole and to create wholeness as we truly and consciously unite with Source, and the greater All That Is.

Go within and be the love that we seek. Rise above the fray and do your part to correct, heal, and resolve all the damage that has occurred while we were off course. Every valid earthly lesson from any earthly lifetime has been about love and the sooner we imbue and be the essence of Divine love, the sooner we can expand and extend our earthly contact beyond the sky.

Our cosmic families are ready to assist us in this grand clean up, dear lighted ones, but first, we must acknowledge and act upon what we know to be true. There is not one species that can save us from the mess and destruction that we have created. As an attribute and promise within our soul blueprint, we allowed for the recognition to also awaken to the healing and clean up that we are finally realizing must begin. We are One with our planet, we are One with nature, we are One with our cosmic families, we are One with our physical bodies, spiritual essences, and our Godliness. We are One with the All That Is. We are One with Source and Source is One with us.

II

Introduction to Path Work

Ascension path work is not something that is accomplished outside of you. Path work is an exploration of all that is within, where your infinite potential resides. Daily path work is all about *you*. The expansive path work you commit to every day will allow you to create a portal through which Universal and galactic wisdom can flow. Moreover, path work will also open the cosmic doorway for your celestial team and family to engage with you with greater ease. Our most ancient teachings tell us that *knowing thyself* is the pathway to all that we desire to create, manifest, and experience. Knowing thyself is the key, and path work is necessary in order to master this unique earthly experience. Knowing thyself is the map, the path, and the infinite road that must be travelled to move beyond what is and what may be.

Awakening

Most of us are no longer satisfied with an obsession for material things for we are finding that such behaviours are creating and reinforcing disconnection within our reality. We are awakening to the truth that we are far greater than our present reality allows us to be. The reality we have been experiencing is an illusion and we are now learning that we created and manifested every aspect of it.

As a collective, we are realizing the level of disconnection that exists and the part we played to create it; however, we are also discovering how vital it is to take greater ownership and responsibility for our reality and our experiences. Accountability is necessary to initiate the changes we need for ourselves, for each other, and for our planet. It all begins right here, right now, and with a purity of intent to know how expansive and Divine we truly are.

When you discover that you are fed up with the lessons associated with greed, disconnection, and fear, you may allow these negative attributes to become the fuel that ignites a fire within you as so many others are doing. There is a massive wave of awakening initiations all over our planet. In every corner of our world, people are waking and sensing a greater spirit intelligence within and recognizing it as a Source aspect of unconditional love. This aspect is what will allow you to experience an entirely new Earthly experience.

From behind veils of illusion, so many people are bursting into their own light essence as they recognize the brilliance that has been stirring within. Each day more and more people are engaging in self-help or self-focused skills to find and activate what truly exists within. This, dear lighted ones, *is* a massive wave of collective enlightenment.

It is time to act in your best interest in every now moment. Know that you are worthy of experiencing the very best and activate the catalyst that will bring about the necessary change. Even if you have no idea what is on the other side of the veil, please trust when I tell you that it is exhilarating beyond words to act on behalf of your spirit and soul. Act with courage and bravery in such a way that it alters all that we know. The chance to truly reengage with life and spirit once again will assuage that ache within you for something more.

We are all being stirred by Source to awaken into a loving potential of our spirit aspect, which aches to be heard, touched, and felt at the deepest level. There is something amazing that exists within each of us and awakening stirs our profound desires to feel a depth of self-love, entanglement with life, entanglement with Source, and the spirit within. As we do so, we will experience the vast power of what resides within the infinite.

Know Thyself

Knowing thyself is the infinite pathway within. The path to self-knowing is unique to each person. The state of being that emits knowingness *is* the essence, and *is* the frequency that *creates*. This is an inspired concept that has long been part of spiritual wisdom and is even recorded in our most ancient texts.

When you create truths that become your knowingness they become a frequency, an essence, and then that influences your state of being. Daily sacred path work can reveal your current truths so that you can discern which truths are ready to be revamped or released and which truths require greater acknowledgement, embracing, and nurturing.

Seeking within to know thyself allows us to escape the mindless floating among the wave of blind masses. Seeking within steers us toward a self-created path of profound spiritual and physical experience. Allow the spirit within to play a more active role in your daily experience and your physical reality will be enhanced as you experience a greater soul merging.

We are multidimensional beings of Divine light, and as we ascend, we will gain access to greater aspects of all that we are and we will merge further into an ever-expanding state of being. These are the mechanics of our personal ascension and as we move further into our Divine self-awareness, our energy fields, our capacity to love thyself, and our innate ability to sense all aspects of our reality, it will naturally flow forth with every moment we dedicate and commit to seeking the spirit within.

Grace

How we unveil the sacred element of grace within is our next level of learning upon the path of ascension. Grace is encoded within every living being, just as love is. We are all encoded with certain aspects of Source and as we move through the various lessons of awakening and ascension, we reveal new attributes, behaviours, skills, and gifts that further enable us to continue in expanded service to the Whole.

Grace transpires when we finally release self-loathing and self-limiting ideas about who we thought we were. With grace, we walk with greater inner compassion and love for the self and all that we exist within. We demonstrate grace in our behaviours expressing compassion instead of judgement. Grace is acting with kindness and patience instead of anger and fear. Grace is acting in full awareness that we are all One and all that we do will reflect and impact *thyself*. When we acknowledge and own all that we are and realize all that we are is enough, perfect, and Divine, we unveil our inner sacredness and allow grace to further unfold.

Grace is a sacred state of being that requires a commitment and devotion to be truly authentic in our own unique spirit and to be of service and light to All. Healing our planet to make it more sustainable within the whole is possible, but it requires that we acknowledge all that we are and all that we can create. All that we are and all that we do is innately linked with Creation. This was our promise in the high councils, dear lighted ones, and it is one that we all made: We offered all that we are to the Whole with honour, grace, and humility.

When we grace our life expression with our authentic and Divine self, we offer all that we are in tenderness, in wisdom, and in the hope that who and what we are will serve in order to allow Source light to enter and expand each of us. Source knows of our perfection. Source knows of our power and profundity to create and manifest light, for it is within us to do exactly this. To be graceful in our own light, graceful in all that we are, for we are an aspect of Divine Source and we would not be here if we did not have the All within to help us overcome all that is blocking our way to healing and ascension.

Love thyself, see thyself as Source sees you. Love your physicality, love all that your body does. Even if you feel your body is imperfect and not functioning well, tell yourself that you are needed and required anyway. Give your vessel the love, attention, kindness, and grace that it requires. Create the state of being in which grace flows from all that you say and do and know it is all an aspect of you and Source stirring within. You are sacred and you are brimming with grace. It is now time to reveal it, for grace is required as we enter these final phases of this profound planetary shift.

Connecting and Community

There is something truly beautiful when people find others with like vibrations and end up creating pairings, groups, and even families. I have held many events, meditations, and gatherings, and I am always amazed and delighted when a group of strangers become interconnected due to the intercession of spirit as it seeks to engage and entangle with our act of communing. The lifelong friendships created on a foundation of deep reciprocal values that feed our desires for improved intimacy with our fellows makes walking this path so utterly worthwhile.

Awakening inspires a greater desire for peace, love, and a sense of community and these ideals will spring forth as we make small vibrational shifts to incorporate harmonic living and eschew self-serving behaviours. Those who are moving through their ascension path work will find great peace in deeper connections with those of like vibrations. Synchronicity brings these like-souled people together into groups and soul families. Each member may discover that they have been serving each other over a span of many star systems and lifetimes. What is different this time is each person will find their way together to develop a greater sense of purpose in their union as they explore their shared soul-purpose and excitement for expansive exploration of spirit.

Love and light are positive and integrative, and they in turn generate greater love and positivity, which in turn ignites our desires to act in loving communion with all aspects of our reality. The more we act from the centre of our being, in a heart-centred manner (thus expressing spirit itself), the more we will see immediate results and changes that loving behaviour inspires. As the rarefied streams of consciousness potentials are sent forth in every celestial alignment, humanity can actively take greater ownership in embracing these offerings by creating group and familial meditations, and storytelling activities to magnify and amplify these Divine frequencies in a truly magical way. Synchronistic experiences will flow and many will experience the complete reversal of illnesses.

With such a Divine connection every day, we will sense and access the wisdom and skills from our ancient lives to assist us in this current lifetime. We will remember how to entangle with our own Divinity. The very act of gathering with Spirit will facilitate our entanglement at a deeper level. As this occurs, we will feel an even stronger desire to entangle with all aspects of our reality experience. The desire for communion is linked to our sense of Oneness and wholeness. As we become more connected, we strengthen our ability to solve many of the problems and challenges that we now face as we attend to the task of correcting the many errors associated with living in great disconnection and disrespect for our planet and wildlife.

As we face a reality that is teetering on the brink of destruction because of aeons of casual disrespect and (not so casual) greed, we will need to tap into the compassion that was awakened during our engagement work. There is much to be done, but much is being done. In fact, since December 21, 2012, there has been a dramatic and positive change in the level of interest about worldly structures that need improvement. Our ecosystem, our political and economic infrastructures, and even our food supply systems are collapsing. Human-built systems tend to be self-serving systems that lack integrity and simply cannot win over the pure love and compassion that we are now seeing expand. These systems must serve and benefit the greater good and the expanding consciousness of the people is inspiring and creating the changes that are necessary.

Humanity's frequency and intelligence are accelerating and there will be no corrupt system that can withstand this phenomenon. Everything in our society *will* evolve to be positive, community-serving, fluid, and free to match the resonance that all the people carry and emit. It simply must, for these are the mechanics of this quantum energy.

Our reality is illusory and all aspects within all that we experience are entangled, so as we shift and adjust what we know to be true, so too shall all other systems shift and adjust. It is an attribute of quantum entanglement. As we inspire one another with our expansive thoughts, ideas, and inventiveness, our societal systems will alter to match with the human frequencies we ignite. Knowing thyself will allow each of us to tap into the inner workings of how energy moves and alters all within its path.

There are many people, from all walks of life, stepping up and acting with heartfelt intent to engage, entangle, and inspire a greater intimacy and meaning within all aspects of our reality experience. Allow yourself to take notice of all these positive changes. There is a greater awareness now because we all desire the promised greater potential of this earthly incarnation.

When we make the personal commitment to connect in a more intimate way with all life around us, we will experience the results of our intent and actions. Committing to knowing thyself is the action part of ascension. In fact, many masters and teachers have explained that this is the key activity that will alter our reality experience.

These shifts in ourselves and in our personal relationships will also influence the way we live. There will no longer be a need for individual housing and many may feel greater freedom and experience deeper value in living within larger groups that serve the purpose and needs of the many. Communal living allows for group sharing of resources, skills, tools, stories, and experiences in an open and generous manner. Communal living will become more common and it will serve as a housing strategy with significant benefits to humanity and for Gaia.

My Introduction to Path Work

I was beset by the darkest of dreams after the birth of my second child. These nightmares left me exhausted, fearful, and confused. I even contemplated suicide — the most tragic and desperate act of separation — as a result. I was utterly lonely, disconnected and sleep-deprived. It was only my two young babies sleeping peacefully in their beds upstairs that kept these thoughts of ending my pain from overwhelming me.

I sought help and met with a family counsellor who prescribed meditation. I had no expectations for any specific outcomes, I was just open to trying anything. I committed to finding a solution to ensure that my babies would get their mother back and so I proceeded. Meditation became an empowering process because it would eventually reveal the shadows that haunted me in my dreams. I was afraid to face my demons head on, but in doing so, I came to understand them, release them, and ultimately heal from the trauma they caused. Little did I know that I had started on the path to becoming my Divine authentic self.

I did not know anything about the realms of spirit and beings that I have since connected with. In that moment, my teams, my spirit guides, and even the celestial sky seemed to align with a Divine offering that set me up with a perfect opportunity to go within and learn about me and my place in the cosmos. I had no more excuses to ignore what was stirring within my consciousness. It was my time to begin.

The kids were sleeping, the house was quiet, and I sat with a gentle meditation song playing in the background. As I breathed deeply, in a way that felt comfortable, I felt a desire to breathe even more deeply. It was as if I had already known what to do. Something inside of me led with every breath. I began to feel a lightness that I now know is a symptom of entering a heightened state of consciousness. The Universe was perfectly aligned to cradle and assist me with my first attempt at inner work and it took only a few minutes before I slipped into a very deep state of meditation and a heightened state of being.

I began an indescribable spiralling in a Merkabah-type of rotation that spun me in all directions and at great speed. I even felt as if I was levitating when I began to sense a being with me. This being was so angelic as she exercised a profound power to execute exactly what she wanted to with a Divine precision.[1]

I learned a lot about myself in that session and it was such a positive experience that I am always eager to continue this vital path work. These profound multidimensional experiences are the reason I have committed my every waking moment to my path. The level of union, love, and belonging within each path work moment is beyond description in its profoundness. It simply does not yet exist here upon Earth, but I have faith that it soon will.

I know I am not alone in finding that our earthly way of life is often confusing, lonely, frustrating, and even harsh in the depth of disconnection we experience here. This reality may seem very dense, lonely, and challenging, but many of us already sense the resonance of our other celestial lives resonating with our personal energy fields. I am so grateful for that one fateful morning that the Universe converged to show me what I had forgotten. I was shown the profundity of what truly resided within. To this very day, I am deeply grateful and blessed for every experience because my cosmic family and angelic guides took me from the darkest place of despair to living in a bright now moment of bliss.

---

[1] For a more detailed description of this experience, please check out my book *5th Dimensional Consciousness*.

III

Preparation for Path Work

When we honour and love all that we are, we will be inspired to create time and space to fill our senses with scents, colours, and symbols that will inspire us at our heart level. An altar is a special zone, a space that is set with an intent to pray, connect, inspire and link with all that we are so we can access our highest, best, fullest, and most authentic self. It is essential that we commit to spending time in this sacred space to engage our guides and cosmic family in our path work. Furthermore, it is vital that we prepare ourselves for this work so that it is a productive effort on our part, ensuring that we do not block our guides from sending us the information and experiences that we need to progress on our paths.

Sacred Space

Create an altar space dedicated to the sacred tasks of communing and meditating. Include specially chosen natural elements that inspire you and enhance your connection with Gaia, your spirit guides, and your celestial teams. For instance, you may place some of the following sacred items in your altar space: crystals, rocks, bark, sand, seashells, positive and inspiring quotes, pyramids, candles, incense, tarot cards, or any other metaphysical tool or symbol that speaks to you.

Celebrate and honour this sacred space, for it will be a sanctuary where you will feel, experience, commune with, give to, and receive from Spirit. It is here that you will invoke the elementals and invite your team to work with the special symbols that you choose. As you learn about the energetic offerings gifted to you, you will be able to imbue more of these sacred essences into your sacred space. As you commit time each day, with intent, to go within and love thyself, you will unveil all the symbols that will guide you on the next phase of your learning and expansion.

Remember, dear lighted ones, this journey is supposed to be fun and playful, so imbue your sacred space with joy. Consciously intend to have fun with every interaction and you will discover how truly magical life is. Be your fullest most profound self. You are worthy of this level of magic, love, and depth to know who you truly are. You will come to know your most expansive self, for you are filled with unlimited potential just waiting to be unleashed.

To our Galactic, Cosmic families, and Source, we offer our deepest reverence and gratitude for your devoted presence and light for our grand journey of human evolution.

Sacred Time

Meditation and reflection are sacred, freeing, and exploratory and they truly do shape your earthly physical reality in every way. Daily sacred time is the intimate connection between you, your Higher Self, your Divine team of lighted and higher-dimensional beings, our living Universe, and, most of all, Source.

Meditation is a Divine and sacred act of connection that will allow you to experience whatever it is you so desire and if you commit to this process of greater self-knowing, then greater self-love will flow forth. This is a time to create a loving inner dialogue with the ego aspect, so that it can feel safe and secure in your exploratory process. This will help you limit the negative busy-mind talk so you are more open to Spirit. Your meditative reflection process is about connecting with all that is Spirit, so purposely intend allowance, self-love, and exploration, and you will experience all that you are meant to.

Set aside sacred time to commune with your guides in your sacred space and commit to keeping this appointment. Before long, you will sense their presence where ever you may be.

Unconditional Love

It is important to be open and fluid with your visualizations, because openness allows for greater self-confidence to be infused within your experiences. Allow your Higher Self, spirit guides, and teams to do what they are assigned to do and gift you with all that they can. They are trying to help you escape the cycle in which you are experiencing the same life lessons over and over. The more open and loving you are going into any meditation and multidimensional experience, the more you will get out of it.

Resistance, lack of self-worth, and lack of trust, only add challenges to your expansive process, creating greater effort and work for your team in getting pertinent information to you. Meditation and daily reflection should be entered with a joyful, fun, and excited energy. This is not a time to let your ego take over.

Grounding

It is important for humanity to expand in awareness of how intimately entangled we are with our planet. In these final ascension phases, we will know when we are not in tune with Gaia, as our bodies will be challenged to keep up with the massive waves of changing frequencies, as Gaia moves into a higher state of being — with or without us. The safest course of action is to engage in parallel expansion work for our own ascension so we can keep up with the changes.

We are all encoded with elements of Gaia and it is vital that we link in with her as often as possible, not only to ground the energies spiralling in the ethers, but also to grow and expand with her as she changes. In the coming months, it will become increasingly important to entangle with our beloved Gaia.

Grounding is one of the ways in which we can link in with the energy system that sustains us, protects us, and nourishes us as we move through these ever-accelerating and profound experiences. Grounding is a very important aspect of the ascension process. It not only allows us to sense what is moving through us, so we can increase our awareness of our own physical vessels, but also allows for greater cohesion during these intense planetary fluxes. Grounding every day, prior to a meditation (and even throughout the day), is an inspired activity that we are well served in including in our daily routines.

Once you start, you will know how vital it is as you will feel the consequences when you do not ground yourself with Gaia. Every new phase of ascension will come with a set of symbolic offerings and noticeable refinements in our personal frequencies so grounding before every meditation will ensure that your multidimensional experience remains enjoyable.

Before I start any meditation, I focus my intent and breathing, linking both with the energy and heartbeat of Gaia. I use a *White Light Prayer* and invocation (found in Section VI) to assist me in getting grounded before every meditation, including group events and private sessions. It is important to always state your intent and centre yourself in a state of unconditional love prior to connecting with the ethers and with higher-dimensional beings and realms. Offering an invocation, expressing your willingness to explore as well as your heartfelt gratitude, will ensure your frequency moves easily within new energetic experiences.

Connecting the Sacred and the Mundane

The level of commitment and dedication to sacred ideals that you decide to imbue your everyday life will affect what you experience and how you experience it. What you put into your Earthly reality will be exactly what you experience and every experience is a beautiful lesson waiting to be discovered. You are your Divine sacredness. Every aspect of you is sacred and Divine, in every moment, in every experience, regardless of what activity you are engaged in. You are always sacred, even when you are carrying out the most mundane of tasks.

Set about your life and create sacred time and space to commune with all aspects of the unseen, for it will unleash a whole new level of experiential wisdom that will facilitate your growth and expansion. Your sacred space is where your most intimate thoughts, emotions, desires, and dreams will flow and it is this space in which you rediscover and remember all that you are in the most Divine way. It is worthy of a little time and attention to create and embellish, for the magical discoveries of you reside within it all, but remember to take a bit of this sacred space with you wherever you may wander.

You are a Powerful, Divine, Sovereign Being of Light and you have the magical ability to alter and shift anything and everything that arises in your life. If you desire entanglement with nature, Gaia, like-minded souls, and your higher aspects, celestial teams, and spirit guides, then know that it will be so.

IV

Ascension Path Work

Each morning, I wake up at 2:02 a.m. so that I can connect with my teams, my higher self, and the myriad of beings who have contracted with me to help me fulfil my soul blueprint. I have discovered that as I expand and ascend, I do not always have to go into a meditative state in order to access my teams. Such surreal interactions are becoming active in my everyday life as I am increasingly focused on an intent to live as spirit in every moment. This is facilitated by the planetary and collective conscious frequencies that enable anyone who is engaging spirit to make these amazing connections much more easily than could have occurred even twenty years ago. Our species is being offered a most profound energetic potential that will allow all beings a clear pathway to spirit *at any time*.

As I walk about my life and move through my everyday daily duties, I have found that I can link-in and connect with my Higher Self and my spirit guides easily and I can even sense when a higher-dimensional being is present. My physical body and heightened senses now alert me when there are beings present. I receive a notice with a throb or tweak in the back of my head or sometimes behind my ear. When this happens, I know it is necessary to achieve a meditative state so that I can connect to receive the message or information that my team desires to download to me.

Sometimes, especially lately, these physical symptoms alert me that my team is engaged in energetic workings behind the scenes and I am merely sensing the residue of the shifts that are activated by this work on either my blueprint or Gaia's blueprint. It is really quite amazing to sense this family support that is always encircling us as they continuously work for the very best outcome for all. This level of Oneness is imbued with a deep-felt compassion and love on every level and it is my hope that everyone will feel just how truly loved, surrounded, and supported we are so that all the acts inspired by fear and separation can finally cease to exist.

All of these lovely energetic subtleties are opening for everyone to take advantage of, for remember, Source, God, our benevolent councils and teams all desire that the path to a lighted life be offered to everyone. All beings are loved, required, and offered the same opportunities for ascension and expansion. It is, however, up to us to create the desire for change. It is possible to have a positive and loving life experience, but it requires action on our part. Path work and the purity of heart to ignite these changes, will help us gain a greater self-knowing and self-love, so that we are able to finally experience all that we planned and designed in our personal soul-blueprints.

There is profound power in path work providing you commit to it daily and imbue your reflection work with an honest intent to *know and love thyself.*

The next subsections will guide you in learning to ground and centre within your heart, Gaia, and with unconditional love so you can be on your way to greater self-knowing, brilliance, and profundity.

Intention Setting

Although a meditation experience can be quite fulfilling if you let go and allow your Higher Self to guide the process, sometimes you have specific issues that you would like to address with your guides and cosmic family. You can determine these issues by journaling about the experiences that you have in your daily life or the experiences that you want to have.

If you are reflecting upon a meditative experience or an experience with someone at work or in your family environment, then you should ask questions in order to determine the root causes of the beliefs that may be causing your distress and thus requires alteration. Ask questions such as:

- ☼ What do I desire to experience in this moment?

- ☼ What do I desire to experience as I move about my life today?

- ☼ How can I sense more of my environment as I move about my day?

- ☼ How can I create loving intent with all beings I connect with?

- ☼ What intention and frequency can I align for myself right now?

- ☼ How may I experience greater love for myself and others in this now moment?

- ☼ What do I intuitively feel about this experience?

☼ Why do I feel this way around this person, and what is this person reflecting to me?

☼ Why am I feeling the way I do when this occurs?

☼ What is this allowing me to know about who I am?

☼ What memory surfaced within this inner dialogue that is requiring me to go a little deeper?

☼ How can I alter what I know to be true so that my daily life experience can shift to a higher thread within my bandwidth?

If you have family gatherings or work experiences that bring out emotions of fear, lack of self-worth, or lack of peace or calm, then take the time to jot down notes in a journal and bring these experiences into your sacred space for exploration and reflection. I have found this process most enlightening, particularly when my guides have helped me find an answer. I have seen the evidence of how I physically and psychically evolved as I worked through and managed these personal human experiences with grace and compassion.

This validation and recognition for our commitment to path work as we serve ourselves, our evolving human collective, and our Universe is so inspiring. So be generous with self-embraces and self-recognition because this is the fuel that will keep you moving forward even when the challenges arise. I like to carry a journal and pen with me when I am out and about because there is always some element of magic unfolding in some way and I do not want to miss a moment of it.

Breathing and Grounding

Before beginning any energy work, it is important to centre and ground. You can then colour, intend, and create the canvas in which you desire to access and experience according to your desires. If you choose to invoke a healing, peaceful intent, or wish to communicate with your teams, these are essential practices to develop and train to enable fluidity and confidence in your cosmic skills that are now awakening.

Visualized breath work is very powerful, and when we imbue our loving intent with creative expression complete with tones and colours, we can thus entangle with our physical vessel to heal, enhance, inspire, and thread our consciousness and wholeness with the All.

Breath work, loving intent, and visualization are not only vital, but also have a great deal of impact when we need to feel balanced, well, healthy, and at peace with all that life is unfolding. Regardless of how chaotic life may appear, we will be able to easily ground, engage, entangle, and realign with God at any moment. For when we intend love and light, we are moving within our Godly essence. This is our Divine birthright, and we have all we need to inspire light and love to create powerful unity and Oneness within, which is then emitted to the All.

Breath-Work Exercise

Breathe deeply three times and visualize an infinity cycle between you, Gaia, and the Universe. With each inhale, visualize Gaia's loving offerings spiralling like light through your vessel and moving in an upward motion through the pillar of light of all that you are. See it moving through your chakra centres, right up to the crown chakra, then hold your breath for five seconds. Visualize yourself spiralling loving intent and entanglement with the Universal Mind and all life within Creation, then slowly exhale imbuing your breath with an intentional loving offering. Watch your breath move in a spiralling motion down through your chakra centres that have now entangled with the Universal mind and its offerings. See them dancing with you in the sands and soils of Gaia all the way down to her loving, sacred heart core. This is one complete infinity cycle of entangled and unionized breath. Repeat this process as often as possible.

It is important to state the purity of your intent and imbue your breath with a heartfelt desire to know thyself, to love thyself, and to walk with God in an awakened state in all sacred work. Sacred communion is heartfelt intent and engagement with Spirit. Mastery is found within your ability to create the stillness and silence needed to enter into an open dialogue with God, for we can then align our intent to the desires of experience and enfold into all of Creation's offerings to us. This is how self-love, trust, and surrender is cycled in any dimensional experience. We create the knowingness that is the indestructible thread, the God-spark that we feel ignited within and this unification and embodiment is the light and link to the All.

Prayer and Invocation

Get comfortable although it is important to ensure your spine is as straight as possible. Breathe in deeply through your nose, focusing on filling your entire abdominal cavity with the pure essence of Source frequency. Visualize golden sparks of Source essence entering your body with every breath and feel yourself connecting with the Divine Source as these sparks tingle and twinkle inside you. Feel the *life is breath* process nourishing and enlivening your cells and hear them whispering to your higher consciousness to wake up and join in their dance of life and love.

Slowly release the air through your mouth, then repeat the inhale-visualization-exhale process at least three times. Breathe in slowly and feel yourself relaxing and begin to visualize the sparks of life creating a serene and peaceful space in your consciousness and allow yourself to be cradled and supported in that space. Feel the love that Source has for you.

Once you are centred, focus in on the sacred heart area, and then invoke your intention and grounding. I use the *White Light Prayer* and invocation (found in Section VI), given to me by a dear friend and colleague, the Divine Kala Ambrose, many years ago. I altered it to fit my specific work and desires and I encourage you to do the same. I use it for every meditation as well as in my daily reflective work. Use this prayer or any invocation that incorporates an intention, a sound, or a symbol that is set and keyed to your frequency. Make sure you express your specific desire at this time.

Prayers and invocations are sacred and have been used in every culture (ancient and modern) and in every realm for all our spiritual work. Prayers and invocations are symbolic intentions that incorporate tones or colours as symbolic tools for igniting an energetic link with your Higher Self, your teams, Source, and Gaia. They can also be used at any time in your daily life to help you realign to a higher frequency when the need arises. Prayers and invocations are also used to ignite a catalyst for change in any area of your life.

Set forth with a heart-felt and loving intention, and imbue your prayers and invocations with a purity of heart, in order to create a resonance for increased potential. Intent creates this potential and it stimulates the changes that need to occur. Intend with love, creative desire, emotional fervour, and a mindset for exploration so that the frequency for what comes back will align with what we send out. These daily prayers and groundings are essential for setting the appropriate resonance to *that which you desire to experience*. So, make it count and have fun!

Desires

As you enter into a Divine experience, you may have two or three immediate things with which you desire resolution, assistance, or guidance. It is important to only bring forward a few topics at a time to focus your intent upon the most urgent issues in your daily life. Remember, dear lighted ones, just because you may want something to occur or unfold, it may not necessarily be what is aligned with your blueprint or it may not be the most appropriate or important lesson in the moment. Trust and allow what your teams offer to you and know that whatever comes your way will be what is in your highest and best interest.

It is also quite lovely to move into a meditative experience without expectation and allow the experience to unfold however it will. Trust in all that you are, for you have the ability and skill to manifest brilliance and deep, heart-felt connections. When you have moved along the awakening process and through the various stages, you will begin to sense that every experience is filled with profound lessons, though some of them can be quite subtle.

Interacting with Multidimensional Beings

Not all Universal beings have the same emotional coding and belief systems that we have been conditioned with, so their behaviour and mannerisms will be based on their level of awareness and soul experience. If the interaction becomes uncomfortable for you, you can telepathically ask them to be gentler as they guide you through a lesson. They may remind you that you have complete ownership and Sovereignty over all that unfolds for you whether you are meditating or going about your everyday life. Be bold. Be clear. Be loving. And be confident about your intent and the path that you desire to experience. What unfolds, will match *your* loving intent.

Daily path work may start off rough or jarring because we have not been taught how to connect and commune with Spirit and our multidimensional aspects and families; however, it's important to commit to the process for it is the path in which you unveil more of who you truly are. There are profound gifts and experiences that unfold as you go within.

Daily path work will allow you to explore and gain greater confidence and self-assuredness. The more you practice and go within, the more you can move about life in a fluid, loving, and confident manner. You create every experience within your awareness. You also create the intent in which you move through your life. Act with the intent to be a loving, kind, and open Divine being and you will meet those who also vibrate in this way, on Earth and beyond. All parties involved in any meditation experience are gifted with the lessons of that particular experience. Suffice it to say that all within Creation will benefit from every experience because we are all One.

You are this profound.

Lessons in Every Experience

Even if you feel as if you have tapped into a void, a great empty vastness, please understand that this is also elegant and beautiful. We are held within all things, even if that thing appears to be empty. There is a reflection and lesson for you to find even in the void. All that you experience is an attribute within the whole, therefore it is all valid, and every experience offers a story. As you are within the All and the All is within you, there will be expansion within all that you move through. Our Universe is not superfluous, so move into every experience as it is a gift from the Divine. Everything, every experience, every being that you experience represents a level of existence that is entangled and enmeshed with you and each carries a profound lesson and insight for your soulful experience here upon Gaia. For even the void is an aspect of Oneness.

When you allow yourself to explore all aspects of your existence, you accept and understand in a much deeper and more profound way that you are within the All and the All is within you. You will create a deeper sense of compassion, forgiveness, and love when you learn that even within the shadow aspects and darkness, you are within the All, the Golden, Divine, and Brilliant shining aspects of You.

Time for Reflection

After you have meditated, you will need to explore and reflect upon the emotions and sensations that came to the forefront during your multidimensional experiences. Reflection work is the time when you can truly expand your state of being, for this is the time to bring your heavenly experience into your present earthly physical moment and ground it into your daily life. So, go within and seek the brilliance and colour of all that you are in expansive new ways. As you grow and expand, you may have a different response and emotional feeling even when you ask the same questions.

As you move through these reflective questions, you will gain a better understanding for these experiences and come to know why you have manifested them. As you gain understanding about all that you are, you will begin to sense yourself slipping into a state of being that resonates with mastery. You will become an expert at gauging what you feel, why you feel it, and how these feelings add to your life's lessons and themes. Try these questions as part of your reflective experience and journal your responses.

- ☼ What do you feel and what made you feel this way? (Anger, hesitation, fear, anxiety, excitement, love, inspiration, pain, freedom, exhilaration, etc.)
- ☼ If you experienced loving and expansive beings, what was their message for you?
- ☼ Did these beings feel like your teachers or family?
- ☼ Did you feel a familiarity with the message you received?
- ☼ Were there objects or symbols used in this experience that you need to take note of, interpret, and expand within?
- ☼ What elements within this experience pops out at you and why?
- ☼ What feelings resonate with you and why?
- ☼ What perceptions have changed as a result of this experience?

You will find that the reflection step will help immensely in your everyday life, as you will come to know the grand design for your life as you gain greater understanding of yourself and of others. The impulses for anger and impatience will be diminished, first of all because you have developed a greater capacity for love and compassion, but also because you know that every experience is an invaluable lesson that contributes to your progress on the path to ascension.

Uncomfortable Lessons

Your team will always guide you in the most obvious, loving, and safe manner. As you expand and master your skills, their messages and lessons will become more subtle, but as you will have grown intuitively, you will have little trouble interpreting what comes your way.

If you experience something that brings up negative or fearful emotions or memories, know that there are always benevolent reasons for this and you will have provided consent at a higher level. In order to expand, we must release all our limitations, particularly those that are fear-based. If you feel fear, identify what is making you afraid and assess the belief so that you can understand it, change it, or release it. You are never given what you are not able to understand, move through, or seek greater wisdom from. Know that all that arises will serve and benefit you. Your team is with you in every moment of your multidimensional experience, so they will ensure your safety and ensure that the lessons are relevant to your soul blueprint and the greater good of All.

Higher-Dimensional beings are innately aware of the rules of free will and benevolence, so they will never overlook them. You will never be controlled or manipulated by any being, unless you designed this within your blueprint so that you could experience it, and then move beyond it. If you set an intention to connect and link in with a loving and open heart, then what you experience will be returned from a loving and open heart. Only the highest beings of light will engage with you. You are a Divine, Sovereign Being of Light, and if there is a situation that makes you feel discomfort or ill at ease, then you can merely ask for your team to bring a lesson forward in a softer or less intrusive manner.

Shadow Experiences

We may be having a loving and positive day and then, when out of the blue, we feel a sense of sadness or even a lack of self-worth. It is important to allow these darker and shadow aspects to surface, as this is the acknowledgement part of the release. It is not always necessary that you know all the details of every dark aspect of your memories that may surface during your path work experiences. Most of the time, we feel these darker emotions because they are a reaction to our energy field being cleared and refined.

You are expanding in your awareness and as your energy field expands with your growing awareness, there will be outdated, limiting experiences or frequencies that no longer fit your new resonance. These limitations and blockages must be cleared. As you expand with confidence in your wisdom and mastery, you will find that it is easier to allow these darker aspects to surface. You will then be able to move through the associated lessons with grace, forgiveness, and compassion for all beings; thus, working through your shadow aspect will become a pleasant and fulfilling experience. You will have plenty of assistance with these tasks, as all those who have contracted with you to aid you in your evolutionary experience love you most profoundly. Once you have allowed these aspects to surface and have learned the lesson about its purpose, you can then invoke with loving intent a new truth frequency that will allow you to realign with an even higher vibration.

Energy is everything and everything is energy. We can ignite our current state of being with love and expansiveness, which in turn generates a positive reaction and frequency experience. What we know to be true about all that we are will be a direct reflection of what our experiential reality mirrors to us.

V

Prayers and Invocations

Prayers and invocations are sacred communions with Spirit that inspire union, healing, wisdom, and soul growth. It is our sacred intent, our actions and loving entanglement with ourselves and Spirit that allow us to unfold as the pure Divine, living, light beings that we are and permit us to experience all that will open to us. Invocations allow us, as masters of our own paths, to initiate a new vibrational engagement and commitment with ourselves, our teams, Creation, and with God. Merely creating the pure intent for our sacred silent time to be present with God, our Higher Selves and teams, is the communion and gate that allows for any and all of God's majesty to be ignited.

White Light Prayer

I am aligned with the highest of beings of light.
As I allow for the benevolence of my highest path, the highest path of
the human collective, and the Universal harmonics in which there will
be a win/win for the All, I am bathed within the golden white light of
Divine Mother Father God Source light.

Nothing but good can come to me; nothing but good can come from
me, and as I open for the love, healing, and assistance from only those
beings in the highest vibrational frequency and those that are
contracted to work with me on my path of ascension and awakening,
May I offer my deepest gratitude and reverence.

For this loving and benevolent interaction and entanglement,
I open the energetic threads of potential for wisdom, love, healing, and
guidance that I may receive here today.

35

May I now see, hear, know, and act within my highest truth.

I claim my Divine expansiveness and unity with All of Creation and to more richly know my eternal loving partnership in co-creation with God.

In Gratitude, Reverence, and light,

Thank you.

Amen, Amen, Amen

Invocation to Ask for Healing

In this moment of now, I surrender into the loving cradle of Creation, held within the loving care of God, so that I may heal, release, and transmute all soul wounds that no longer serve me in this now moment.

For the greater good of the All, may I release and heal _____ that stirs within me. (Identify the specific key intent key, i.e., a wound, injury, or desire you wish to transmute)

I ask for healing, for love, for guidance, and for the light of the Arch Angels, Master Jesus, my celestial teams, Spirit Guides, and Source for their expertise in guiding me beyond these limitations and fears so that I may experience the profundity of all that I am.

As I surrender this limitation and fear, I reveal more of my limitless life potential and I unfold and bloom with unconditional love for all of Creation.

I love. I trust. I surrender. I accept. I allow. I acknowledge. I receive. I honour.

I AM THAT I AM.

Invocation to Claim Your Birthright

I stand before you now and surrender into the profundity of God and of Creation, so that I may claim my birthright with pure intent to reveal my sacred wholeness. Allow me to see, hear, know, and feel my Divinehood with you, God, and my connection and link that can never be severed or extinguished.

I acknowledge and accept that I deserve to be loved in all ways by you, by Creation, and I am now ready to experience it and ground into it. I deserve to live in wholeness and unity and I deserve a new sense of knowing in which I can begin to co-create with mastery light within this Earthly reality.

For the greater good of the all, I trust and honour in all that unfolds, for I know the heart of Creation is held within and I embrace all Divinely offered gifts. I claim this right to be loved, healed, and ignited with the energetic skills and wisdom that will best serve my path and that of Creation.

I am a Divine, living, light being of profound potential. I am worthy of all that I seek. I know You gifted me with this life and my desire is that I serve and honour You in all that I am able to create.

In all that excites me, I deserve to be here in this moment of self-discovery, self-love, and offering to Creation as I invoke my most loving and expansive self. I ask for unconditional love, guidance, wisdom, and support as I live every moment with an open heart so that I can express the purity of my love.

In this healing, may I live with forgiveness and compassion in all ways, to all beings and most importantly with myself.

Invocation of Surrender

I surrender all that I have known to be true about who I am, so that I may unveil my limitless Divine, living, light self. I yearn to feel an inner belonging and sense of love with You, God, so that I may co-create with you the myriad of multidimensional aspects that show me how to entangle with You. I crave cosmic freedom, unconditional love, and the knowingness of love in this life. I desire to create ownership and presence within these powerful and profound truths so that I may experience and express unconditional love towards myself and others.

I surrender into all that You are, so that I may own the highest version of all that I am and reflect this to Creation in this Divine light experience. I live with a sense of unwavering trust in all that I am embedded within. I surrender all that stirs as darkness and fear so that I may now see, hear, know, and live with clarity and truth about my unlimited potential. I surrender into my own quantum sea of love and hold true the light, the wisdom, and the compassion that allows for unconditional love to flow through me. I emanate with pure white light from the sacred heart centre of all that I am as my new truth, for it allows me to experience the love, unity, and wholeness that are my birthright.

Assist me in this profound invocation of surrender so that I may know my Divine, loving, whole self. Assist me in this profound revelation to truly own all my spirited potential to heal the wounds that have held me in limitation. I desire to know You, God, in the All, for then I will truly unveil new loving aspects of myself within it. I am capable of this Divine request of love, exploration, healing, and grace, for it is Your grace that allows me to move in the ways that I desire. I accept and allow all experiences to add to my wisdom and healing. I walk boldly forth upon my lightened path of self-awareness, self-love, and self-honour as each loving truth is reignited with the love of Source within me.

In the deepest and most profound way, I express my reverence, gratitude, and love to Creation and all beings within it, for all lessons that unfold provide me with greater wholeness, sense of self, and inner love that are my pathway to inner peace.

In loving still presence, I surrender, I claim, I accept, I honour all that I am and with all that I am gifted, I receive.

Amen, Amen, Amen.

Sacred Temple Teachings

Sacred Temple teachings invoke a loving and Divine union by calling upon all that you are as a Divine, living, light being to access Universal wisdom in order to move, to ground, to act upon, and to use to recreate God's many Heavens. There are myriads of invocations one can create to provide guidance and assistance in engaging with energetic Sacred Temple teachings. These teachings show us how to bring Heaven unto Earth.

Sacred Temple teachings allow the open channel of the pillar of light or the spherical ball of light that we are to ignite into remembrance the already held information from within. These profound electromagnetic interactions, termed *quantum inter-play*, exist when our co-creative teams, family members, celestial friends, or any being you call in, become a part of your activation for remembrance and knowing. As we spiral and move through Creation and co-create profound multidimensional experiences that shift our earthly reality, we become able to expand these teachings to incorporate renewal and recalibration to the infinite array of human social challenges that we regularly face. Sacred Temple teachings allow those who so desire the opportunity to open to the Divine within, to entangle, invoke, engage, expand, act, behave, and be in the presence of your highest frequency potential, thus altering and shifting the All.

Creating Your Own Invocations

When creating your own sacred invocations, the most important tip is to be pure within your heart to what it is you desire to alter, manifest, or transmute. Remember that your Higher Self and Divine teams know what is most relevant and applicable for you in the order of what is most urgent within your blueprint. Have trust in their skill, your skill, and then be grateful for all that unfolds.

The orchestrations that are involved in any one invocation are complex, but know that there is nothing that God is not able to manifest on your behalf. You will always receive what is the most relevant and purposeful — always. Remember to ground with Gaia, offer your *White Light Prayer*, call in those that you feel are resonant to this invocation, and offer your gratitude and reverence within all energetic work. Imbue colour, tone, and playful imaginings into the invocation. Trust and know that you will always create what you require to grow, learn, and love in the way that your Higher Self directs.

VI

Our Divine Destiny

Our human experience has given in to belief patterns that ignite hesitation when we begin our journey toward spiritual liberation. But we are here to tell you that all paths are Divinely orchestrated per the will and intent of every being. Know that every being is lovingly guided and cared for by richly intelligent teams and councils. These teams and councils are directed by the Highest Self of every being. Our wings of exploration, dear lighted ones, are aching to stretch the vast infinite horizon, and we must surrender to the cosmic wave of love and light to truly begin the next phase of our unification adventure.

All things are possible in these times of lighted cosmic offerings and higher dimensional living, but you must surrender to the limitless flow of Creation. As you yield, not only will you sense it, but you will be shown the loving wave in which you ride. This Divine offering exists in your moment-for-moment atunement with your presence, silence, and unconditional trust that you are indeed an important part of this magnificent orchestration.

Envision that you are standing at the altar of this incredible cosmic wave of love. The altar comes alive with each breath of loving intent you take to know thyself, and with each intentional breath, you are Divinely co-creating in the name of Mother Father God. Creation evolves in cycles of orchestrated design and endless flowing love, all of which is Divinely gifted by the Creators, and then managed and maintained with precision by groups of beings and by conscious awareness. We come to know that our daily, moment-for-moment breath is within a grander Divine cycle of evolutionary loving growth, and in this knowing, we can fully surrender into the flow of the Creator breath that carries us to the design of our Higher will.

Trust in the All

Our unique offering to Creation is unconditional trust. Our faith in Creation allows us to participate in whatever brilliance may unfold. Despite the challenges that may surface, we now understand how to masterfully navigate our journey by refining our choices and being open to the lessons bestowed within each experience. You will always be exactly where you need to be and receive exactly what you need when you live with an open heart and unwavering faith in Creation. Trust that you are supported and cared for in every way.

This lush consciousness weaving that supports us is infinite. This multidimensional web is that in which *All* experience resides. It houses the Divine and fuels and supports all within it. All life is supported through that which it was created. All aspects of life within our known Universe is supported to the extent that all possibilities in life can co-create, experience, and fulfill. We have yet to remember the full extent to which we are Divinely loved and supported. Our consciousness awakening will ultimately allow us to surrender into all that unfolds.

The River of Life

Imagine there exists a Divine river that flows with golden potentiality. This river meanders in and around the Divine embedding that is always available to you to surrender into. This Divine *River of Life* is woven within the breath of life, so inhale deeply and make it your own. As this profound essence moves through your vessel, you can infuse it with your creative free will and imagination, thereby yielding Divine majesty. You are the alchemic master and you can lovingly command your cells to ignite new growth, heal your organs, and activate the DNA wisdom that exists within your infinite design.

As you free yourself from all things that hold you back, breathe into the gifts, opportunities, and heightened flow that is held within this *River of Life*. This *River* is the breath of Mother Father God. It is inspired from the center of our Universe, the most pure, loving emanations of what we know to be the benevolent Creators of Universal life, profound majesty and all that loving Spirit is. Love is the All. Spirit is the All, and Mother Father God are within all aspects of you. Existence truly is this way and must be for it to support and maintain the vast diversity of life that is present in this Universe. We flow within such cycles so that we can entangle, engage and evolve into future now Universal cycles, threadings, and experiential potentials.

Imagine now that you allow your vessel to commune with your breath and your higher intelligence (the Divine Sacred Mind). Then as you project light within your breath to commune with the breath of Mother Father God, you open a portal of new Divine unfolding potentials. As a Divine alchemic master, you have the power to ignite the spark of the golden encodings available to you. Your ability to commune with the breath of All That Is, and the golden sparks of Divine offering, makes the *River of Life* flow as easily as the purity of your intent to swim within Its blessings. This is entanglement in the most loving and unified way. There are no other tools required.

The breath of the Divine is spiraling within you now, supporting your every move and every dream. It can be used as your anchor to which all miracles are made manifest. Your heartbeat and the heartbeat of Mother Father God are One. This union is the fuel that inspires a loving orchestration of purity and creativity.

Divine Loving Flow

Masters and shamans have long since known that the *River of Life* is the breath of Spirit, the breath of Mother Father God gifted without condition and available to All to soak within. It is a loving flow that can live through you from your Divine Sacred Heart Center and then be offered in your own unique way to Creation. This visualization concept has been offered in every one of our meditative teachings. It is also referred to as the infinity cycle of breath (See Chapter IV Breath Work Exercise), grounding and aligning you with All That Is, and our Divine Goddess Gaia's energetic flow.

This elegant and powerful flow is the source of endless inspirational energy. It is gifted with ever changing light encodings that nourish the development and expansiveness of all that lives and breathes within Its essence. This energy *can* be felt within all things because this essence is the living pulse within Creation. These golden bubbles of consciousness are embedded in the All to provide constant support. They are endless particles upon infinite particles of Spirit essence, and are all sewn together within this immaculate energetic realm. It is within every being and every dimension.

Flow is found within breath. Flow is the surrender, with unconditional trust that you are a Master. As you surrender, you understand that you are cared for, supported, and loved by the Divine Mother and Father who carry you in Divine loving flow. Flowing entanglement begins and crosses the crucible of intention at the center of your being: The Divine Sacred Heart. This is your treasure chest of all potentials; it is the limitless portal to All of existence. The purity of your intent, your colorful imagination, any lofty dreams and your knowingness that all life flows through you guide you into higher dimensional living.

There is an infinite well of potential swimming within the hologram that is every particle of life. We are unified, we are One, we are threaded in this Divine entanglement and our bedding is the golden bubbles of consciousness in which we inspire life to unfold. We entangle and sew our breath, with the Divine breath, the seeding of consciousness and potentiality so that we can continue to flow within the evolutionary river that will carry us into perfected frequencies and realms. Breath is life, breath is love, breath is flow, breath is giving, breath is receiving, and breath is the Divine gift that nourishes us in every way. It is an integral piece of our higher dimensional wellness and wisdom that can anchor and expand our consciousness experience in limitless ways.

A New State of Illumination

The breath of life, the river of life, the sustenance of existence is the bedding to which all consciousness exists within and why it was recognized as the ignition to all awakening, enlightenment, inner peace, and well-being. The remembrance of our Divinity, dear lighted ones, is the allowance of our illumination. Allow your light to be all that it already is. Allow your light to shine forth in your words, your actions, your intentions to walk with a lighter step and see what is mirrored to you in return. We create, we imagine, and we inspire every aspect of our experience. What we desire to come to life for us is entirely of our own design and making. Imagine, create, and as you breathe your next breath know that you can begin to infuse pristine color and light waves of your unique imaginings, and inspire new particles of Divine encoding into loving flow and activation. Then you can revel in exciting musings of sacred play with our benevolent planet and Universal family.

Love, light, and flow within the Divine is within you right here, right now, this breath, the combined loving essence in balance, in unity from the Divine Mother Father God, and gifted with heart felt intelligence beyond our imagination. If you imbue this unique vision within all breath, your multidimensional self will be fed in a loving and balanced higher dimensional way. Your next breath is the essence of the next, and the next, and the next and you have limitless skill and wisdom to infuse it with your unique signature creations. Surrender with unconditional trust that you will be shown, you will be guided, you will be loved into a new state of being, a new state of illumination for it is available to you within every breath.

Create your daily Sacred Self-love affirmation and intention statement in the space provided below.

VII

A New World

In these accelerating times, we are being steered toward our innate beauty, and we are being guided to fall in love with the new, expanded version of All that we exist within. In these accelerating times, however, we can sometimes feel overwhelmed by the information received from the plethora of channels, teachers, and speakers now offering their gifts. When we are overcome with these feelings, it can make the next step on our path difficult to see. So, what can we do to honour the gifts being offered to us at the same time we maintain a sense of clarity in these accelerating times?

Honour Your Inner Temple

To increase our spiritual discernment, we must return to the heart. Our Divine Sacred Heart, the power center of our Inner Temple, is the home base of our unfolding spiritual path. It is the starting point, return, and funnel for all transformative energy that magnifies and amplifies all manifestations.

Love, excitement and joy are sourced through your Divine Sacred Heart. It is here where we connect with the Heavenly threading and entangle with Mother Father God, and it is here where we return to in our grounding breath work. Your Sacred Heart is the window and portal to all the joy and excitement that emits from you and through you. We are meant to live every moment of life from our heart center.

Find Your Authentic Voice

Have you been inspired to seek your authentic voice and speak your authentic truth? Have you felt the urge to identify your authentic gift and nurture it in order to serve and to live in excitement and joy? You may have wondered how this new cosmic reality will inspire a new earthly reality. You may have also wondered how you can play within these new realities to live a more joyful, loving aspect of who you are. I am here to tell you that a new world experience is here and now. For you to come alive within it is the free will and creative genius that each of us were gifted with.

As your path unfolds, and as you center in your Sacred Heart you will come to truly know your authentic joy. Staying focused in your heart will protect you from living the vision of what others direct or wish for you. You will come to know what your new world experience offers you and what you offer it and the All within it.

We are on a journey, dear lighted ones, to discover how to be a shining version of joy and authenticity in this life now. Just breathe and you will know that your unique center point is your pure knowingness of God within. To live in purity of this will reveal to you every gift, every offering, and the unique authentic encoding that is within you. You are the breath of life gifted from God. Within breath you can ignite, nourish, heal, and infuse new life. So, just breathe and guide your Divine Sacred Heart to center as this is where all Divine treasures reside and so too shall it be revealed to you.

The authentic voice, the inner gift and spirited musing that is yours to offer is like no other, nor should it be compared to others. You are a blessing uniquely designed with distinct talents, and this earthly reality is your platform. It is the stage that is beckoning you to bring forth your authentic gifts so that we can co-create the most prestigious world offering to date.

Tuning into Your Unique Vibration

In my own journey, I found a great technique to help reveal my authentic voice. I came to understand that All things carry vibration, but that vibrations vary in their frequency. My technique consists simply of speaking words and phrases that resonate with the highest of vibrations thus truly deepening my sense of self.

Eventually I was shown a vision of myself as an angel of tone, and the elegance and beauty of sound struck me in a way that I will always remember. I saw myself within this Divine Heavenly energy, and as I felt the movement of the angelic essence, I began to align my earthly frequency with it so that I could open a new portal of potential I had not known, but innately felt spiraling within me. Humans are naturally inspired by music, color, and dance because they can emulate other realms. It is our way of engaging in heavenly play and enacting our unique Divine decree.

In a flash of an instant, my perspective of who I thought I was, was forever shifted. I want you to know that despite the subtlety of these energetic offerings, they give you the opportunity to attune to higher frequencies. The more you attune within who you are, the greater in alignment you'll be to unveil your authentic spirited offering to Creation. This is how we can be inspired by Spirit and our Divine Sacred Mind. As we work toward our highest path, we experience the highest energetic bleed through of energy that ultimately assist Creation in raising the vibration of all.

In exploring some of my gifted visions and inspired musings, I began to record my playful inner workings with sound, toning, and intention. There is a mathematical movement through which tone and intent combine to create the color and manifestation in all things. The Divine Sacred Mind and the Divine Sacred Heart are the engine and navigator within the Inner Temple that inspires not only flow, but intent, beauty, compassion, and all twelve God Rays, so that what you emit is of the highest vibration that not only serves the greater good, but can also create and manifest beyond your wildest imaginings. This is how the highest of realms create and co-create with one another. One authentic voice, with another authentic voice and the majesty of spirit unveils.

The more that I began to play and enjoy the tones and sounds I created, the more that my inner Divine-self came forward in a fluid manner. It was my inner spirit coming forth demonstrating my authentic gift and spirit, and designing a fresh Heavenly contract. In many of my playful toning sessions, I could feel specific tones aligning me with ancient memories inside temples, and upon cosmic waves of consciousness. I intuitively knew that the sounds I created were being sent into a higher vibrational thread to co-create in a new way. The sound particles were alive and they were happy to be breathed into existence with Heavenly intent and passionate love to be as free as the wind that carried them.

This has truly been a magical remembrance for me and one that feels authentic in its unveiling. It was an innate offering within the entire multidimensional version of who I am becoming. I am now sensing, with greater authentic toning play, that these tones are assisting with the translation and processing of refined multidimensional higher vibrational wisdom that is now being activated and downloaded within my etheric field. I am playfully stretching my light field so that I can truly step into the dynamic unique version of me that I designed. And by design, I am filled with excitement that I get to play and co-create with Gaia and other soul family members. Tones are vibrational ignition packets, and like any other Divine gift, they are embedded within our Inner Temple encoding waiting to be awakened.

Revealing Your Sacred Gifts

Your authentic gifts are within you, dear lighted ones. The gifts within your Sacred Temple allow all other gifts to be known and felt. When you feel excited about an offering, you have activated something powerful; follow this excitement, for it may allow you to unveil a profound path of Heavenly rediscovery. This is the way in which Heaven upon earth is created.

Remember that as you awaken more fully and integrate your soulful self, your gifts will deepen, and they may even shift all together. You must remain open to how your path twists and turns, for it is meant to do just that. This is how mastery often unfolds and why surrender and self-love will open the door to truly create greater atunement to what your excitement is showing you. Whether your excitement reveals color, wildlife, nature, song, dance, movement, or energy healing, know that this is just the beginning. As you project higher frequency vibrations, you will be gifted with sparks of Divine remembrance that can take you upon a new path within the cosmic field of light.

A New Way of Living

We are meant to be in joy, in light, and in excitement about all that we are becoming, and our sense of play will shift unlike any other lifetime upon earth. Tell yourself that this is okay. Dive into your new joys thereby inspiring every moment you return to center to be still within your Divine and beautiful presence. Our new way of behaving, of playing, of being the new illuminated version of who we are is meant to feel different, new, and even unusual at times.

We are beginning to be the higher versions of all that we are and it will inspire us to explore, express, and live authentically in the moment-for-moment now within a new set of Heavenly orders unique in this lifetime.

There is no other expression of a Universal being that is just like you, nor is the energy that is gifted, like yours. There is no other spirit or point of view like yours. You have an authentic voice, and you have authentic gifts that allow you to be exactly where you are. Our uniqueness requires each of us to authentically own who we are, and to create excitement about our new 5th dimensional version of all that we are. New reality experiences begin with inspiration, excitement, and playful action to manifest the burgeoning light field of a new world.

Be Inspired to Play

If you desire a new earthly reality then one must begin anew. Let go of societal cues, expectations, and old designs. Instead, choose to play within the energetic offerings available to us now. Play with Divine tones, sounds, and unique language within your DNA and etheric field by setting a playful intention and inspiring it into action. You are every part of the quantum equation and you can ignite your reality in any way you desire. Without joyful play, we cannot explore the possibilities available to us thereby experiencing only what has always been.

As you act upon every playful intent, you will be inspired by new gifts being presented for you to entangle with. We are living within higher dimensional encasings and vibrational threading that will support our every move that is imbued with unconditional trust, joy, love, and creative design. Allow your authentic Divine angel of light to come forth and play and be seen, and to shine forth in the way you know exists within.

Let go of what others may think, or desire for you, for this is your journey. Remember that you wanted the grandest version of yourself, fully integrated within the infinite number of you that could offer it all. All of your gifts, all of your parallel lives, all of the fiery stirrings within, are your birthright to emit and begin anew right here, right now. So, play. Be joyful, sing, dance, play with the intentions of love, project loving light, and infuse your profound love with limitless offerings from the Divine and watch the magic unfold right before your eyes.

Be Your Authentic Self

You are a Divine inspiration, dear lighted ones, and there is no one else like you. You are authentic in your love; you are authentic in your voice and how you use it. You can only activate the energetic genius if you are willing to step forth and be fully you. Your higher dimensional life is right here, it is now, and you are swimming within the Divine Heavenly blessing that is you. You have an important role in this Divine dance, so it's time to come forth and play with the Heavens.

You are immersed with love at every moment. You are worthy of love and it is safe to play within your heart-felt joy. You create this new world order, this new world vibrancy of light and playful beginnings, and make no mistake about it, it is awaiting your engagement and your unique creative touch.

Your spirit is calling for you to step up, step forth, and be the light that you are, for there truly is no one exactly like you and your gifts.

This is a truly sacred path of reunification with the Holy Mother-Father-God within, and how we ignite our remembrance of this opens the limitless potentials for peace, love, and harmony within the All.

About the Author

Joanna Ross was born and raised in Victoria, British Columbia, Canada. At a very early age, she was infinitely inspired by the minute subtleties of life around her. Taking in the immensity of even the smallest aspects of life, it was this internal stirring to seek and know that aligned her with a series of naturally progressing events that spurred her profound spiritual awakening. Joanna is passionate about understanding the true human potential within the vast and infinite aspects of our Universe and how to unveil what resides within each of us for greater gratitude and aliveness. In her twenties, she moved to Vancouver, British Columbia where she worked in a variety of public and private sector jobs until her seeking finally led her to metaphysics.

The birth of her second child triggered a series of dark, soul-wrenching dreams that were the catalyst to the ultimate unfolding of a grand understanding of our human potential and the role she was invited to take on at this time. She experienced many profound synchronistic events that triggered the need for even deeper research, self-reflection, and self-discovery as she was inspired to engage with and grasp the enormity of what we all truly swim within. Her expansive study, inner knowingness, and the incredible multidimensional adventures she has experienced, have become her life's passion and destiny. This remarkable path of planetary and human ascension paves the way for the most profound self-discovery and it is in this demarcation that the miraculous will unfold.

Joanna now lives out her passions for Universal Unity as an Intuitive Visionary, Esoteric Teacher, Ambassador for New Earth, and Public Speaker. She calls Calgary, Alberta her home where she loves to play and learn with her three young children, create artwork, and embrace the joys of entanglement and unity. Joanna's primary passion and life expression is to be a student of Creation. In utter gratitude and reverence for this earthly experience, she is devoted to inspire, to share, educate, empower, and enlighten those who desire to understand the profundity that resides within us all. It is her joy to offer guidance to help others discover their infinite human potential. May you all experience solace, light, and your innate gifts within as you walk this incredible path to a 5th dimensional unfolding.

For more information on ascension, enhancing multidimensional living, private intuitive readings, or public speaking engagements, or to book a *First Contact Symposium* in your city, please tune in and explore our 5th dimensional offerings on our website.

Universal Light Wisdom & Healing Centres

http://universalunity.ca

Universal Unity

Higher Vibrational Learning and Ascension Offerings

Understanding the multidimensional aspects that allow humanity to tap into the heightened frequencies of our celestial family, and enhance lightship engagement is fuelled by a rise in human intrigue and the desire to engage more fully with our celestial teams and family. The auspices of Source through various Councils within Creation have planned everything. It seems that Gaia and humanity are right on track for cosmic expansion. Ascension offerings allow you to gain insight into this profound wave that has washed over our planet, what it means for our everyday living, and the potential for each person choosing to tap into these incredible frequencies.

Ascension offerings allow you to know more about the process of lightship engagement and what they have to do with our evolution. Extra-terrestrials, lightship sightings and engagements, first conscious contact, and human evolution is entangled in the most profound and quantum manner. What does this mean for you and how do you create the essence of unity and intimacy with all aspects of life and Creation? Learn how to entangle with your true multidimensional reality existence and even learn to tap into the presence to help our celestial teams provide guidance to every human being. Learn how to manifest the life you truly desire that is fulfilling in every way. Go within and learn how to deepen your innate skills so that you are able to entangle with your celestial teams, spirit guides, the Higher Self, all humanity, Gaia, and Creation to experience the magical essence, the profound synchronicity that is our 5th dimensional human potential.

Climb aboard as we step up into a glowing 5th dimensional reality. Joanna's passion is to create, inspire, and build expanded understandings and concepts about what human and planetary ascension is and how it affects every aspect of our reality. Joanna will help you understand what that tickling sensation to find answers means and how to bring these triggers to the surface and ultimately understand the grander soul blueprint.

Private Intuitive Sessions

http://universalunity.ca/private-sessions/

These are truly profound times and if you sense that our reality is shifting, then you will not want to miss this *master activation* and higher learning presentation. Awaken aspects of your soul blueprint and unleash your Divine purpose to come *online*, so that we may entangle and engage with Source, Creation, and our celestial family once again. Our current Earthly, planetary, and collective changes are all attributes of the refined frequencies that are being streamed to humanity and Earth for the ascension shift in the coming years. Tune in now to align for these incredible shifts and 5th dimensional potentials.

Enlightenment, awakening, ascension — whatever you want to call the profound changes we see in every aspect of our reality — is all about humanity tuning in to the unlimited potential to be our most infinite and Divine self.

Joanna Ross

Joanna — intuitive visionary, esoteric teacher, public speaker, author, and Ambassador for Universal Unity — has been on her ascension path after an awakening occurred soon after the birth of her daughter. Her intense journey of self-discovery, mystical unfolding, and reunion with greater conscious awareness, as well as her spirit guides and celestial teams have brought an ever-heightened awareness to the Universal energies that rule our reality experience. These are all stones in the path that have lead us to these incredible here and now ascension offerings.

Universal Unity Radio

http://kcorradio.com/KCOR/Universal-Unity-New-Earth-Consciousness-Joanna-Ross-KCOR-Digital-Radio-Network.php

Join our *Universal Gathering* every Saturday morning from 11:00am – 1:00pm Mountain Time for expansive ascension, multidimensional discussion and dialogue as we tune in with our Universal teams to learn more about all that we are and all about the Universe we exist within.

Children of Light

http://crystallinelightchildren.blogspot.ca/

A revelation and Divine stirring from my own path work inspired a new blog about the crystalline light children born in these times of ascension. Find ascension teachings, musings, interviews, and more inclusive of children.

Private & Group Events

http://universalunity.ca/uuevents/

Joanna offers private and group ascension, higher vibrational enlightenment, self-empowerment, first conscious contact, enhancing multidimensional communication, and other trans-formative events to guide participants in gaining in-depth insights and wisdom about Universal energy, human potential, and the grander perspective about our Earthly experience.

We are being prepared in every way to entangle, engage, and inspire a new level of human/Creation intimacy and it begins with our journey within. Join Joanna and her team in the many expansive offerings as we all gather within our soul families to assist in healing humanity, healing Gaia, and inspiring a new level of engagement within our Universal experience.

First Conscious Contact

http://universalunity.ca/first-contact-symposium/

Successful *First Conscious Contact* events are the first of its kind and will allow those aspiring for a deeper entanglement with all aspects of Creation to engage in a new forum to gather and expand together. This event can be brought to any group location for the most incredible interactive experience that offers the primary and foundational attributes to understanding the grander scope of our multidimensional existence and preparations for first conscious contact.

Prepare for what is being offered from the Divine, for it is your birthright to unfold in this way. There is so much more to the human experience and our Earthly existence. Time to tune in and dance the dance to expansiveness.

Joanna Ross

Other Books by Joanna Ross

Available from Universal Unity Publishing

http://universalunity.ca/books/

5th Dimensional Consciousness

Profound Ways to Awaken Your Potential and Align with Future Contact

This first high-vibrational offering from Joanna L. Ross — intuitive visionary, esoteric teacher, public speaker, author, Ambassador for Universal Unity, and global radio host — shares the key understandings about the shifts and changes we all see, experience, and know to be true as Gaia moves through planetary ascension. This new energy is created and triggered from within. The pineal gland, along with various other physical components, creates a portal to experiences that will enable the expanded growth that is required for us to ascend, with Gaia, from a 3rd to a 5th dimensional resonating frequency. In this ascending process, we release, shift, and alter all that we are. We let go of old beliefs and unlock our true, hidden potential thereby allowing us to unite and build the bridge to the greater cosmos. Your ascension begins here.

The Dance with Creation

The Power of Three

This book is the third higher frequency offering to those within humanity that are ready for a deeper entanglement, a deeper meaning, and to explore our potential to create a lighter way of existing within the diversity of Creation on our rapidly transforming planet.

The Dance with Creation will inspire those who set out to explore the grander elegance and self-discovery of what resides and entices from within. These energetic and soulful stirrings are the synchronicities of your limitless potential and will always guide you to a greater cosmic unfurling. May we tickle at the heart level and empower you to know your infinite presence, and your power to refine and ignite new paths that show you how utterly engaging and profound every breath can be. Gain greater insight and knowingness for what elements of Source reside within and how to activate greater entanglement with your Higher Self, your spirit guides, and your celestial teams.

Made in the USA
Lexington, KY
16 May 2017